Patience Wright

Patience Wright

America's First Sculptor
and Revolutionary Spy

Pegi Deitz Shea

illustrated by Bethanne Andersen

HENRY HOLT AND COMPANY ❋ NEW YORK

❋ *Thanks to Jeff Dwyer, Elizabeth O'Grady, and Mary Azarian*
for "introducing" me to Patience Wright, a fellow Jersey Girl.

—*P. D. S.*

Henry Holt and Company, LLC, *Publishers since 1866*
175 Fifth Avenue, New York, New York 10010
www.henryholtchildrensbooks.com

Henry Holt® is a registered trademark of Henry Holt and Company, LLC.

Library of Congress Cataloging-in-Publication Data
Shea, Pegi Deitz.
Patience Wright : America's first sculptor and revolutionary spy / by Pegi Deitz Shea ;
illustrated by Bethanne Andersen.—1st ed.
p.   cm.
ISBN-13: 978-0-8050-6770-5 / ISBN-10: 0-8050-6770-1
1. Wright, Patience Lovell—Juvenile literature. 2. Sculptors—United States—Biography—
Juvenile literature. 3. Wax figures—United States—Juvenile literature. 4. Spies—United States—
Biography—Juvenile literature. I. Andersen, Bethanne, ill. II. Title.
NB237.W75S53 2006   730'.92—dc22   2005021696

First Edition—2007 / Designed by Amelia May Anderson
The artist used gouache and pastel on Arches buff paper to create the illustrations for this book.
Printed in the United States of America on acid-free paper. ∞

10 9 8 7 6 5 4 3 2 1

With love to Audrey Longo Adamko,
another strong single mom

— P. D. S.

To all who are moved after listening and study
to choose the right and are lucky enough to have
history prove them right

— B. A.

*L*ondon, England, already had a thriving wax-sculpting industry in the late 1700s. So in 1772, American-born Patience Lovell Wright moved across the Atlantic Ocean, and her sculpting business soared. But when British cannons soon threatened the American colonies, Patience entered another business: Spying. Her secret messages about British plans helped colonists win the American Revolution.

As a child, Patience Lovell could not have dreamed of becoming a spy. Still, her unique upbringing gave her all the right skills. Born in 1725 in Oyster Bay, New York, Patience was raised as a Quaker by her parents, John Lovell and Patience Townsend. Quakers believe that God lives in everyone, no matter their religion, race, politics, or gender. The Lovells followed a vegetarian diet and didn't wear leather. Patience ate such food as apple dumplings, puddings, and peas with sage and onions. She was used to being different and she became proud of it.

Most important for Patience and her eight sisters was that Quakers believed women should have rights and education equal to men's. During Patience's time, most girls did not attend school. However, Patience and her sisters Rachel, Deborah, Rezine, Anne, Sarah, Martha, Mary, and Elizabeth learned to read and write as well as their only brother, John.

When Patience was four years old, her family moved to Bordentown, New Jersey. There, she discovered her talent for sculpting animals and figures. She and her sisters shaped wet flour or clay, then painted their sculptures with dyes they made from plant extracts. Soon, Patience's talent rose above that of her older sisters'.

In the 1700s, most girls married in their teen years. Not Patience. She was incredibly independent. Patience waited until she was twenty-three to marry a much older man, Joseph Wright, a landowner and cooper. He spent weeks at a time managing his far-off properties and working in Philadelphia, but Patience didn't mind because he disapproved of her art and her independent ways.

When her husband died in 1769, he didn't leave Patience any money. Being resourceful, Patience decided to support her children with her art. At the age of forty-five, Patience moved her family to Philadelphia to live with her widowed sister Rachel Wells. Patience found city life exciting and diverse, and she rebelled against some of the quiet Quaker ways. Though she kept her faith in God, she began to eat meat and to wear colorful clothing.

Patience's acceptance of animal products now allowed her to work with Rachel, who ran a small wax-modeling business. Patience loved working with the soft substance, which was made from boiled animal fat. She could shape wax more quickly and easily than clay. Wax let her form realistic faces with animal hair, and wax absorbed dyes more evenly and vividly. The sisters could make their own wax from blubber or buy it cheaply at the city's bustling wharves. Patience had found her artistic medium.

With financial support from Francis Hopkinson, a lawyer and artist friend, Rachel and Patience soon opened their own studio. They often worked in their shop's front window to attract attention. The wealthy class, who had seen or read about popular wax shows in England, became fascinated with the sisters' art form. The customers wanted three-dimensional framed portraits, busts, and life-size wax versions of themselves and loved ones.

Unlike most sculptors who used plaster casts, Patience sculpted from live models or from memory. Customers often mistook her finished life-size figures for real. People spoke to the figures before they noticed the glass eyes and wax noses!

To create life-size figures, Patience used wire, string, papier-mâché, and wood to make the armature, or frame, for the trunk and limbs. She supported the body with an iron post screwed onto its back. Patience could clothe the frame in the customer's own favorite garments, or she could sew a new outfit. Usually, the wax head was shaped separately, then attached to the body with strips of papier-mâché. Details on the wax hands included tiny hairs, veins, and pink fingernails.

Patience and Rachel set up permanent exhibitions, or waxworks, in Philadelphia and New York City. Their portrait subjects included George Whitefield, a southern evangelist; John Dickinson, a patriotic news writer who published articles attacking King George III and Parliament and who helped frame and sign the U.S. Constitution; Francis Hopkinson, who later signed the Declaration of Independence; and Cadwallader Colden, lieutenant governor of New York and a close friend of Benjamin Franklin.

The northeast winters slowed business and made the wax hard to shape. To warm the wax, Patience kept pieces of it between her thighs. While the customer posed, Patience blindly shaped the wax face under her skirts. Then, like a wizard, she'd pull out the wax head to examine it. If the bust needed a major change, back under her skirts it went.

This technique shocked many gentlemen and ladies. But Patience had become the best wax portrait artist and she was in demand. To set her customers at ease, the quirky, outspoken Patience entertained them with funny stories and political opinions. Patience chatted easily, especially with politicians, who sat still for hours while she sculpted their likenesses.

The cold winters also made the sisters seek business elsewhere. They toured the southern colonies, demonstrating and selling their work. During the winter months, Patience's children visited with relatives or operated the Philadelphia or New York studio. The children—Joseph, in particular—were becoming artists themselves.

But while the sisters were away on a tour, disaster struck. A fire in the New York studio melted almost all the wax figures to be sold! Rachel and Patience had to work tirelessly to re-create the pieces. Ironically, the fire actually made the sisters *more* famous. It brought them publicity, and newspapers hailed the new sculptures as superior to the originals.

Patience and Rachel toured the northern colonies in warm months. In Boston, Jane Mecom, Ben Franklin's favorite sister, befriended Rachel and Patience. Jane urged them to open a studio in London, where Franklin was representing the American colonies. Rachel preferred to run the Philadelphia business, but adventurous Patience jumped at the chance to live abroad. She sailed for England on February 3, 1772. Her children stayed behind for the time being.

Patience had hardly abandoned America; she carried the colonies' causes and desires in her heart. In London, she discovered that her days of discussing politics and opinions had only just begun.

Settled in a neighborhood near the king's palace, Patience attracted the English royalty as customers. Ben Franklin had sent letters of introduction on her behalf to lords, ladies, and Parliament members. In gratitude, Patience made Franklin a bust of himself. Franklin's bust became so popular that Patience and Rachel made copies, which sold quickly in America and France. Returning from Franklin's home in Paris one night in 1781, Patience was nearly arrested for having Franklin's "real head" in her possession.

In London, a young American painter, Benjamin West, introduced Patience to the artistic community. West was appointed historical painter to the king. Royalty often posed for both West and Patience at the same time; he painted, while she sculpted.

By May 1772, Patience had begun receiving praise. The *London Chronicle* called her "remarkable" and "ingenious." Her business prospered. A year later Joseph, Betsy, and Phoebe Wright joined their mother and immediately involved themselves in the family business, sewing costumes, painting, and sculpting.

The wax studio flourished with well-known customers. Patience became especially close to William Pitt, first Earl of Chatham, and to the historian and author Catherine Macaulay. Patience called Pitt a guardian angel because he stood up for America in Parliament.

Throughout the summer of 1773, Patience was invited to Buckingham Palace to create wax busts of the king and queen. In the Quaker tradition, Patience treated everyone equally. She called the king "George" and his wife "Charlotte." (Actually, she called the king "pharaoh" behind his back!) Patience used these meetings to debate King George about the American colonies. She urged the king and lords not to wage war.

The year 1773 was also the year of the Boston Tea Party. The colonists had started revolting against England. Patience found herself in an interesting position to learn and pass on secrets to colonial leaders. Parliament members and new military officers chatted with Patience while they posed. Patience led them into revealing secrets by offering *wrong* information, which they immediately corrected.

But Patience and other Americans were now being watched closely by the British. Rather than mail her letters to the colonies, she depended on messengers to deliver them. As America and Great Britain fast approached war, England jailed many Americans, intercepted all written communication, and limited travel and trade with America. How could Patience send her information?

As she'd done all her life, Patience relied on her art. She had often made copies of famous busts, like Franklin's and Pitt's, and shipped them to Rachel to sell in America. To mount the busts on a base or a full-length figure, Rachel would stick her hand inside the head. So Patience hid her messages inside these hollow busts. Rachel received them and immediately sent the messages to members of the Continental Congress in Philadelphia and other patriots in the northeast.

Rachel Mills
Philadelphia

Before and during the fighting, Patience Wright's secret messages covered a range of actions by Parliament, royalty, and the military. Early on, they relayed that Parliament was cutting off trade to starve the colonies. Some messages named the government officials in the colonies who were taking bribes from the British. Other letters described the number of guns, cannons, and soldiers that England was shipping and where they might attack.

As is true for many spies, especially during wartime, not all of Patience's information was accurate or reached the right people at the right time. The English suspected her of passing their secrets. As a result, British informants may have purposefully given her wrong information. Nevertheless, Patience continued corresponding with American leaders during the war. And she helped free and shelter Americans escaping from London jails and "hulks," or floating prisons.

Late in the war, Londoners were no longer fond of Patience "the patriot." She sailed off to France several times, where wax sculpting was new and where Franklin was America's ambassador. The Treaty of Paris ended the American Revolution in 1783. A year later, Patience received a letter from George Washington, the commander in chief of the colonies' forces and future president of the United States. Washington wrote Patience that he would be honored if she would make his wax portrait.

Unfortunately, Patience died in England in 1786 before she could sculpt Washington in person. And only one of her sculptures—that of William Pitt, Earl of Chatham—remains as an example of her fragile art. The life-size figure stands in his crypt at Westminster Abbey in London.

Patience Wright's talent, independent spirit, and initiative lived on in three of her children. Joseph painted George Washington's portrait and designed America's first coins. Phoebe and Elizabeth continued the family business of waxworks. Phoebe married the painter John Hoppner. Elizabeth married Ebenezer Platt, a political prisoner her mother had helped to free. The Platts returned to America in 1780 and set up a waxworks in the original New York studio on Queen Street.

Patience Wright gave America its first female model of international artistry and political action. Her example, unlike wax, will last forever.

Author's Note

Had the word *feminist* been coined in the mid-1700s, Patience Wright would have been a prominent role model. She and her sister Rachel established art studios in both Philadelphia and New York, then the diplomatic and business capitals of our colonies. Patience likely became America's first international female entrepreneur when she opened a studio in London. Although a female artist was rare enough in that day, a woman who passionately pursued her career and marketed her own products was unheard of. Widows both, Patience and Rachel also raised families—without the modern conveniences that make our lives easier today.

Patience thrived during an exciting time in American politics—when colonists broke free of English rule in the late 1700s. The colonists had long been revolting against English taxes and laws they thought unfair. England would not allow the colonists to have a role in its government, yet England did not honor the colonies' local governing of themselves.

Patience, as a Quaker, was against war at first. She joined Ben Franklin, William Pitt, and others in arguing for peace. When the colonies declared independence on July 4, 1776, Patience did not have trouble deciding to serve America, although she still kept up peace initiatives throughout the long war.

After the war, many patriots and soldiers were rewarded with American land. Patience Wright told her sister Rachel that she wanted her body to rest in America. Rachel, New Jersey Congressman Thomas McKean, and Ben Franklin were in the process of obtaining land for Patience when she died suddenly in London. She was buried on British soil.

A year after her death, the young American poet and fan Joel Barlow wrote about Patience in his poem *The Vision of Columbus*:

". . . See Wright's fair hands the livelier fire control,
In waxen forms she breathes the impassion'd soul. . . ."

Time Line PATIENCE WRIGHT AND HISTORY

1725 ❋ Patience Lovell is born in Oyster Bay, New York.

1729 ❋ The Lovell family moves to Bordentown, New Jersey.

1745–48 ❋ Patience travels often to Philadelphia to visit her sister Rachel.

March 20, 1748 ❋ Patience marries Joseph Wright. They have five children in ensuing years: Mary, Elizabeth, Joseph, Phoebe, and Sarah.

1756–63 ❋ The French and Indian War, a territorial dispute, is fought by British and colonial troops against the French and their Indian allies.

1757 ❋ Ben Franklin appears in Parliament for the first time as a representative of the colonies. He will play this diplomatic role— in France and Canada also—until his death in 1790.

March 1765 ❋ The British Parliament passes the Stamp Act requiring all colonists to buy English paper and to pay a tax on all printed documents, newspapers, and pamphlets. The colonists riot and boycott British goods. The act is repealed in March 1766.

1767 ❋ Parliament passes the Townshend Acts that, among other things, tax colonists on lead, glass, tea, and other goods bought from British merchants. Colonists riot.

May 7, 1769 ❋ Joseph Wright dies shortly before the fifth child, Sarah, is born and then adopted by one of Patience's sisters.

1769–70 ❋ Patience moves her family to Philadelphia to join her sister Rachel in the waxworks. The women open a New York studio and tour the colonies.

1770 ❋ British troops kill five colonists during the "Boston Massacre." The Townshend Acts are repealed.

February 1772 ❋ Patience leaves for London and sets up waxworks. Soon she begins passing military and government information to Ben Franklin and other American leaders.

1773 ❋ When Parliament passes the Tea Act, colonists revolt against it. Dressed as Indians, they dump cargoes of tea from British ships in port; this became known as the Boston Tea Party.

1774 ❋ Parliament passes the Coercive Acts (also known as the Intolerable Acts) and the Quartering Acts to punish colonists. In September, the First Continental Congress meets in Philadelphia.

April 1775 ❋ Fighting with British soldiers begins in Concord and Lexington, Massachusetts. In May, the Second Continental Congress meets in Philadelphia and establishes an army for the United Colonies of America.

July 4, 1776 ❋ The Declaration of Independence is signed; Franklin is a drafter and signer. War continues.

February 6, 1778 ❀ Franklin negotiates an alliance with France, whose involvement helps turn the war in the colonies' favor.

Summer 1781 ❀ Patience travels to France and stays in Paris until the following summer.

1782 ❀ In Paris, Franklin helps negotiate peace between the colonies and England. They sign a draft of the treaty in November.

September 1783 ❀ America and Great Britain sign the final Treaty of Paris, ending the war and proclaiming the colonies independent.

February 25, 1786 ❀ Patience Wright dies.

Bibliography

Adams, Adeline. *The Spirit of American Sculpture*. New York: National Sculpture Society, 1923.

Alberts, Robert C. *Benjamin West: A Biography*. Boston: Houghton Mifflin Company, 1978.

Bacon, Margaret Hope. *The Quiet Rebels: The Story of Quakers in America*. New York: Basic Books, 1969.

Bolton, Ethel Stanwood. *American Wax Portraits*. Boston: Houghton Mifflin Company, 1929.

Marks, Mickey Klar. *Wax Sculpturing*. New York: Dial Press, 1963.

Newman, Thelma R. *Wax as Art Form*. South Brunswick, N.J.: Thomas Yoseloff, 1966.

Sellers, Charles Coleman. *Patience Wright, American Artist and Spy in George III's London*. Middletown, Conn.: Wesleyan University Press, 1976.

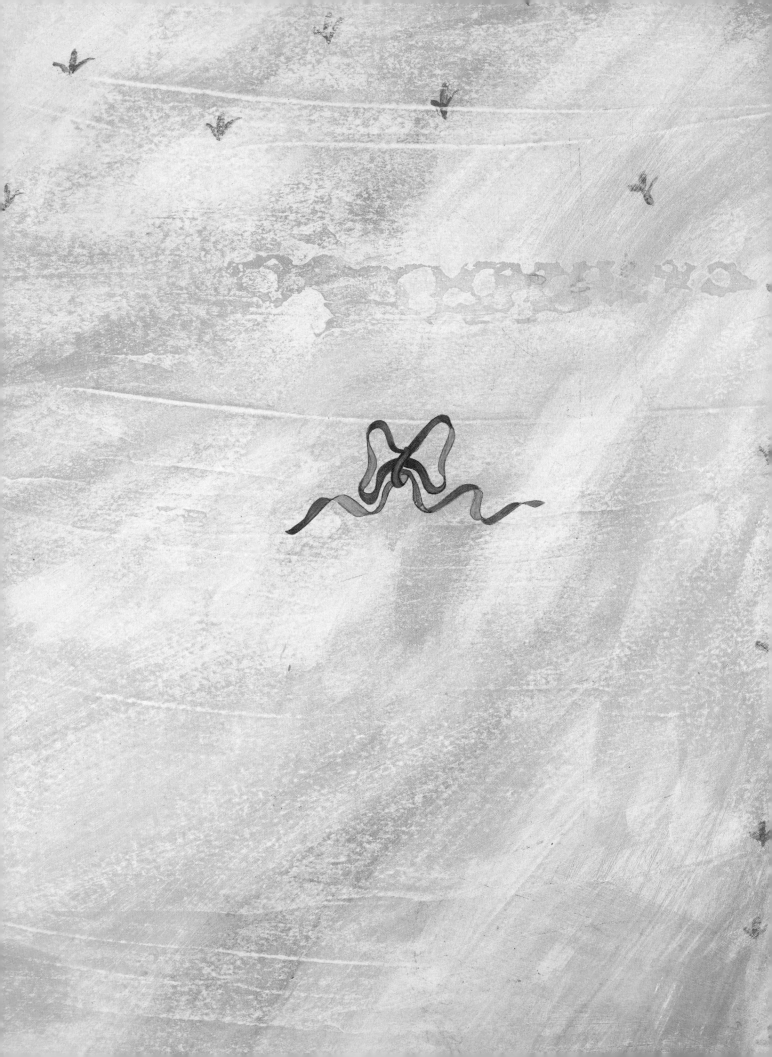